I0624259

Also by Gjertrud Schnackenberg

Portraits and Elegies

The Lamplit Answer

A Gilded Lapse of Time

The Throne of Labdacus

Supernatural Love

Heavenly Questions

St. Matthew Passion

ARROWSMITH

PRESS

St. Matthew Passion
© 2024 Gjertrud Schnackenberg
All Rights Reserved

ISBN: 979-8-9904050-1-1

Library of Congress Control Number: 2024911008

Boston — New York — San Francisco — Baghdad
San Juan — Kyiv — Istanbul — Santiago, Chile
Beijing — Paris — London — Cairo — Madrid
Milan — Melbourne — Jerusalem — Darfur

11 Chestnut St.
Medford, MA 02155

arrowsmithpress@gmail.com
www.arrowsmithpress.com

The Sixty-Second Arrowsmith book
was typeset & designed by Ezra Fox
for Askold Melnyczuk & Alex Johnson
in Baskerville fonts

St. Matthew Passion

Gjertrud Schnackenberg

Contents

A Rising Minor Sixth

A Rising Minor Sixth

Put out my eyes, and I can see you still
                                    -Rilke

I try to pull away, but can't,
My coat drawn halfway on
And hanging crosswise in the back,

The empty sleeve fallen aslant,
Brushing the floor — I have to leave,
It's time, I've set

The afternoon aside for "taking care
Of things" — my scribbled lists
Of valueless, inconsequential errands,

Rounds of chores, and unavailing tasks
I can't put off, all things forgotten
Instantly as soon as taken care of.

But haunting me if left undone.
I have to leave. But when I try
To make my hand reach for the door,

It doesn't move. As if it isn't able to.
As if I had *forgotten you, Jerusalem.*
As if I could. Instead I stand

Arrested at the door, held in abeyance
By the music I left on.
Erbarme dich.

A rising minor sixth unseals the sound.
The violin, engulfed
By what has happened, brings the room

Into another state of being. A seventh sense.
Its aria, self-crucifying, brief,
Is trying to extend

A wordless vocal line.
As if the violin caught sight
Of bonfire-lit Jerusalem,

A small midnight procession,
Roiling torches, shouted Greek.
The sight of Jesus, bound, and shoved ahead.

The sight of Peter, trailing far behind.
Then halted in the dark,
Because *we cannot lift our feet or set them down again*

Without the help — of God — a sound
As if the violin has seen
Nothing as sad in all of Israel,

Even with Jesus fallen on his knees —
Nothing as sad in Israel as the sight
Of Peter, from afar off, following.

I sense the room behind me,
Holding still, engrossed,
As if the room is listening

Because the brushwork of the bow
Is given over to the darkest
Beauty that *b minor* ever touched,

Intent on finding, fastening, F# to D,
In tensile gossamer,
As if the heart's-leap

Of a rising minor sixth
Could be enough to mend
What's happened here.

A leavetaking that no one
Would have wished for,
Wanted, willed.

The *Passion*'s flutes, which shrilled with malice,
Taunting Peter at the bonfire
In the palace courtyard, suddenly are stilled,

Gone dark, cut off, and lowered
In the players' hands
Because they've seen that he

Went out and wept most bitterly.
Peter, who said an hour ago that he
"Would die for him." But now —

But now remembering the store
That Jesus set in him.
That valuing.

Stockstill and lowering my coat
Out of respect because I'm standing
In the presence

Of his wild tribulation, while the violin
Consents to shoulder this,
To stay with him, to take it on,

As being all the violin can do.
But what is worth the doing,
Given this.

Given that the tower Peter claimed
That he would build
Has come to nothing

But a scattering of massive, half-cut
Blocks of stone
Abandoned on a quarry floor.

Only enough for building half a tower.
The other blocks he needs
Still hidden, uncut in the cliffs.

Yet he can see that his messiah has begun
To climb a tower
He built himself, to climb alone.

The *Passion*-sound, from balcony to balcony,
From Thomaskirche to here:
But if my love for you could only help —

I have to leave. Instead I stand stockstill,
As if I'm physically unable
Not to hear it to the end.

As if there's nothing I can do
But stand and listen
To a rising-falling in the treble clef.

As if there's nothing left on earth
For me to do but stand and listen.
As if listening could help.

The *Passion*-sound

The *Passion*-sound

I used a stairway which nearly had ceased to exist
-Anna Maria Ortese

It's unmistakable, the *Passion*-sound,
As if the winds and strings believe
That God, high in the dark, is listening.

A dark of sound that generates its own
Terrain and clime and meteorology,
Engulfing us among the nameless voices

Calling back and forth
Across the rooftops of Jerusalem,
Come ye daughters, help me, help me mourn —

Any page the score is opened to,

Any passage, any part, lies opened

To its heart, and in its midst —

Far-seeing woodwinds, flutes of prophecy,

The voice of the Evangelist

Drinking injustice to the dregs, the plight

Of treble oboes, childlike, naive,

But He has done us only good —

The alto dark of oboes

Questioning the loneliness

Amid the wondering strings:

Does God experience His Creation? This?

Even a fragment, overheard
In a rehearsal, taken up
And quickly broken off, is broken off

As if thrown down, its thoughts
Too great a burden to be borne,
But taken up again by players

Who refuse to leave the *Passion*'s
Call for help gone unresponded to,
Refuse to leave

Its questions torn away
And hanging in the air,
Unanswered, unresolved —

A sound so charged with care
It turns its listeners
Into involuntary witnesses

And inadvertent lookers-on
And random passersby, persons
Anonymous, indifferent, unaware,

But stalled by what they've heard,
Caught up, cut off
From their immediate concerns,

And changed, from who and what they were,
To shocked participants,
Gebracht, drawn in

By instruments believing they were born
For this, by voices born to call
From Thomaskirche's balconies,

What shall I tell my soul —
What shall I say, when the appointed hour
Has come and gone,

When each and every one is called upon,
And even God
Is called upon, to mourn.

Workshop Instruments

Workshop Instruments

> *For as soon as the wind goeth over it, it is gone,*
> *and the place thereof shall know it no more.*
> -Psalm 103:16

Queried about the fluency and grace and speed
Of his unerring keyboard touch,
Songlike, *cantabile*, and unimpeded

By the fingers-thumbs conundrum
Of accomplished amateurs
And gifted students he befriended,

The *Thomaskantor,* Bach, too plagued
And busy and exasperated
To go into it, replied

That anyone could play the way he played —
If they would work as hard — and said,
"It's not remarkable,"

And said, "The instrument will play itself,"
As if he had his harpsichord to thank
For his renowned, unparalleled legato.

"Ceaseless work, analysis, reflection,
writing much, and endless self-correction,
that is my secret" —

But nothing in surviving documents,
No pencilled words,
No stray remarks to colleagues

Scribbled in the wake of casual conversation
In rehearsals with his
Local church musicians,

Caspar, Gottfried, and Cornelius —
No written evidence
Comes down to us, that Bach was ever given

To discuss the secrets of the instruments
He wrote for — nothing indicates
He ever found it odd or striking,

Worth remarking on,
That hollow, manmade objects,
Carved in Leipzig's local workshops,

Understand the *Passion*'s inward,

Haunting, intimate

Experiences of God —

Perhaps too occupied to mention how

He thought it possible

That empty wooden vessels

Carved from boxwood, rosewood,

Maple, satinwood,

With twisted joints and blowing holes

And gaping breathing-vents,

Could have the insight to express

God's mortal passion to be understood.

Herzliebster Jesu

Herzliebster Jesu

The fairest order in the world
is but a heap of random sweepings
-Heraclitus

Even as a child, I saw the prism

Of *b minor* lying broken in the staves

Of the chorale,

Herzliebster Jesu, was hast Du verbrochen? —

A child's question, trying to deduce

The shape and angles

Of a shattered crystal prism

From a heap of splinters

Shining in plain sight —

What has He ever done, what trespass,
What transgression — I saw
The accidental sharps'

Jagged, chromatic dissonance
Embedded in the words
Beneath the black light

Of the ultraviolet harmonies
Scanning the question in the hymn,
Seeking a trace, a trace — discovering

Only the presence
Of the heart's blood shed at death —
I stood with them, a child

Among the congregation risen to its feet,
Risen as one, acknowledging
Music beyond the reach of ritual,

All standing in the beauty
Of the dark, blood-smeared chorales,
The music taken up, experienced, felt

In the first-person singular and plural —
A gathering in memory
Of the savage damage

To a human heart, where dissonances
Tear the staves apart,
And yet major to minor cleaves

Among the keys' black signatures
Of intimate compassion —
I stood with them among

Suspended intervals, augmented sixths,
Descending minor thirds, and saw
Colors appearing on the wall —

Harmonic changes visible,
Familiar, strange, where Bach
Had rearranged the spectral order

Of the colors, part by part,
To underscore that *All is changed* —
Though little did I know

That all was as it was,
Or know the world has always been
The way it is, or know

People have always done
What people do — I didn't know —
I only knew

Creation as the predicate
Of pre-existent love, and knew of love
As a conclusion long ago foregone —

I only knew unbroken bonds
The way the colors cleave,
Both fused and set apart,

And only *there* so clearly without volume,

Mass, or tangibility.

Yet not illusion. Not illusory.

"The kingdom isn't something you can see,

Or gesture toward, to say

It's here — or here —"

Spectral — except I felt the weight

Of C#, pausing in the tenor line,

Grow palpable,

A shadow in my chest

That gathered mass and heft and edge

As if the accidental sharp

Were driven clear into the pulmonary cavity

At Golgotha, then wrenched back

Like a spear —

What trespass, what transgression — a sharp

Existing only in the weightless harmonies,

Transpiercingly

Reflecting light above the word

For "misdeed" — *Missetaten* —

Finding me the way

A splinter that I've searched for, couldn't find,

And gradually had forgotten,

Pierces me.

Builders of Instruments

Builders of Instruments

And tongueless I can still pronounce your name

-Rilke

All lost to us, Bach's visits to the sawdust realms
Of Eichentopf, and Hoffmann's
Carving studio,

The *Kapellmeister*, seated in his weekday
Black wool greatcoat fringed
With fine-grained particles

Of woodwork meal clinging
Magnetically to him, *aus liebe*, out of love —
The quintessential,

Stalwart, barrel-chested, bedrock Lutheran,
Charged with the maintenance
And oversight of all repairs

To Leipzig's churches' inventory stock
Of winds and strings (no powers could defend against
The scuffs and scars and broken pegs

Of instruments trundled on carts
From church to church,
Winter and summer, year by year) —

The local titan seated on a sawhorse workbench,
Pressed for time, but blowing air
Into a double-reeded mouthpiece —

One of Johann Heinrich's

Innovative oboes —

Testing out its novel obbligato

Voice of love, as if to ask the instrument,

What is a holy sound? What constitutes

The sound of holiness?

Surrounded by a scattering

Of cases for the violins and flutes,

Left opened on their hinges to expose

The concave imprints

Of their absent instruments,

Like empty tombs —

Bach's faithful confidence was never shaken,

That local workshop instruments

Were capable of following His steps

As far as Golgotha, to join

The women who had followed Him

From Nazareth,

And stayed with Him, and stood,

And from afar off were beholding —

And yet I've seen

The instruments without their players,

Lying idle, stilled,

Scattered across the semi-circled

Chairs during a break in a rehearsal —
The flutes and oboes, left behind,
At rest along the ledges

Of the music stands, as if they're only good
For propping pages open.
I've seen the violins, shut in,

Mourning the waste, and filled
With shadows to the brim,
As if they're unaware

The players who abandoned them,
When parted from their instruments, can only
Saw the empty air with empty hands.

Aus Liebe

Aus Liebe

Each of us must bear our part

\- Chris Zimmerman,
The Bruderhof

I need a heart of bronze for hearing this,
And not the lost wax melting off
Beneath a molten pour of sound

When, out of love,
A solo flute appears —
Appears, whether or not I've grown

Sick of the world, sick of the things
That people do, sick of the ache, and in the end
What difference does it make

That *He has cast out every sickness*,
Given what has happened.
Given this —

Why summon from the air the oxygen
That's needed for a last
Outflowing breath

Above a slowing pulse? And what
Can flutes accomplish? What do
Flutes have the ability to do?

Why draw a breath
Not even deep enough
For blowing out a candle flame

That cleaves *aus liebe*
To the wick it carbonizes
As it writhes, why take

Repeated shallow sips of oxygen,
And why array
The fragile respirations of a flute's

Expiring *appoggiatura* sighs
Against the site of massive violence
And abandonment at Golgotha,

And why apply circular breathing
To a frail lament that seems
To breathe itself into existence

For my joy and pleasure,
While Thou must suffer —
Though it's true

That, lifted to the lips, Bach's flutes pursue
The anguish to its source,
With tongue-assisted embouchure,

The way a tongue will touch,
Draw back,
Then touch again

A welling gap of sudden blood
No gauze can stanch
After an aching truth

Is torn out by the roots —
I take a breath, and move
To turn the music off, but stop myself,

Relenting, giving up
Because it's clear it doesn't matter
Whether I concede

The miracle that flutes,
For all their frailty,
Can overflow with truth

When human beings are themselves
Incapable of saying it —
The truth that *each of us*,

However frail, *must bear our part* —
The truth that he has held
The lead weight of your heart,

And weightless notes are capable
Of weighing it
Before they vanish off

To go wherever music goes
When nobody
On earth is playing it.

Bethany

Bethany

Du lieber Heiland du/Buss und Reu
- Picander, Recitativo and Aria

When all that we would give remains ungiven —
Then *f# minor*, flutes,
And second thoughts

Whose slowing steps grow heavy, heavier,
Among wind-carried particles
Of myrrh scattered across

The threshold of a room
To which a pair of flutes returns
And touches down,

Tugged down by gravity
From veering altitudes
And swooping heights

Of righteous accusation, shrill rebuke —
The flutes, who only live
On borrowed breaths,

Are touching down with aching steps,
Brought back to earth,
Brought down

By the compression-depth and shock
Of unforeseen departure. His.
An alto voice appears

Amid the circling of wordless flutes,

To speak for them,

To offer their duet,

With shamed remorse and bitter rue,

As a belated gift —

Requital — recompense

For how they'd blindly witnessed,

Blindly missed,

What Jesus thought

The world was worth,

One moment

At a modest gathering

Among unvalued persons
In a leper's house, in Bethany,
And Jesus seated. Soon to be unseated.

His men, standing around him,
Having grown
So used to Jesus' poverty

They overlooked it, couldn't see
That there was anything
On earth that Jesus needed.

A waste, they said, by which they meant,
Wasted on him,
Excoriating her, the woman

Who had seen in him that love
Without which life is little more
Than empty errands,

Rounds of endless chores.
Burdens lifted up,
And set back down —

The woman who had seen
The prodigality of the Creation
Pouring out around them

Where they stood — the kingdom,
Profligate, and present
In the room,

And in its midst,

His royal destitution.

For which she broke the seal

On her jar, and poured an overflow

Of fragrant oil in her palms

To press it to his hair.

And Jesus, breathing in the scent

Of burial spices,

Aloes mixed with myrrh,

Could see an empty shelf of rock,

A vacant shroud,

A quadrangle of blue

That opened out onto the scent

Of scattered boulders,

Ancient olive trees.

The petrichor of opened earth

Beneath a gardener's rake at 6 a.m.

The shining blur

Of lightning-scrubbed, limestone Jerusalem.

And Magdalene approaching, unaware

That he already stood awaiting her.

Cataract Surgery, 1750

Cataract Surgery, 1750

I come to the end — I am still with you
- Psalm 139:18

Bach at the end was blind, his hand
Touching a wall to balance where he stood,
A bandage of black linen

Wrapped around his eyes after the oculist's
Experimental surgeries had failed.
— Put out my eyes, and I can see you still.—

I look up, and it's dark outside already,
So much later, harder
Than I could have guessed

To turn the music off and step away

And put an end to this,

Taken aback

To find that I'm still lingering,

Still standing here

With lowered coat

Among the nameless voices,

Softly now, *We call to you,*

Rest Thou my Jesus, softly rest —

The room, reflected in the gleam

And soundless black

Of window glass,

Remains intact, with everything in place,
Just as it was.
The books and tables,

Chairs and lamps, untouched
By the upheavals in the music,
Offer up no evidence,

No trace, of what the winds and strings,
Entwined with human voices, saw
In following the *Passion*'s

Grave descent from key to key
And world to world
Among the music's apparitions

Where a cold red sun
Was nailed to the West, and Jesu's head
Was hanging on his breast,

And at his feet, Mary to Mary cleaved —
For all the power of harmonies
To move the laws

Of physical reality aside,
For all the slowing-down
Of oboes pulsing underneath

The flutes' anxiety,
For all the heart's-quake of the violins
Within the *Passion*'s tumbling walls —

For all that's happened here —
The perpendiculars
Of ceiling, walls, and floors

Are still aligned, still sharp,
And undisturbed.
The door's rectangle, still rectangular.

Yet this is where the *Passion*'s
Come to rest
Within *c minor*'s sealed walls,

Where we *sit down in tears*
Among the stones,
Where *Mary and the other Mary* sat

Across from where the tomb was sealed —
The women who had stayed with him
Beyond the end,

But knew they had to leave
Before the sunset's horizontal line
Of brilliant red collapsed

And bled away into the twilight
At the place of burial
Where love is not a gift

But something meted out to us
Like punishment
And unearned grief.

World, go away. Geh aus.
World, disappear,
And leave me here with him,

And leave me
Where the women couldn't see
The world had gathered there,

The exiles, captives, prophets, slaves, and scribes,
And psalmists, rulers, counselors,
Daughters of Zion,

Teachers of the law, musicians, holy men,
And all the company of human suffering,
Were seated there with them

Among the stones outside Jerusalem.

And all around the sealed tomb

On every side… the crowns of kings… were heaped.

It's finished, dark, it's late,

I have to leave — except —

Except a fleeting oboe,

Stepping through the ending

Of the *Passion*, lifts

A single step

Within the staves, from B to C.

A brush of sound.

Then swiftly gone.

An oboe, nameless, bodiless, and footless,
Blind, alone,
Disworlds itself, intent

On moving past the end, intent
On following footfalls
Of steps another takes for us.

Nearly unheard. I have to leave —
But having overheard a fragile oboe
Drawing near its purpose —

A spirit passing through a wall, unhurt —
And without any feet can go to you —
My footstep stalls, midair, unable to.

NOTES

Page numbers refer to the *St. Matthew Passion*, BWV 244, vocal score based on the Urtext of the New Bach Edition, Bärenreiter, BA5038a. All German quotations are from the libretto by Picander, the pen name of poet Christian Friedrich Henrici. Translations of the libretto are taken or adapted by the author, using various English versions.

A Rising Minor Sixth

Put out my eyes, and I can see you still: Rainer Maria Rilke, *Poems from the Book of Hours*, New Directions, 1975, p. 29, tr. Babette Deutsch

If I forget you, O Jerusalem, let my right hand forget its skill: Psalm 137: 5

Erbarme dich: *SMP*, Part 2, aria 39 (47), p. 169

Truly, 'tis not in the power of men to lift up their feet or to put them down without the gods: From *The Words of Ahiqar*, The American Foundation for Syriac Studies website

And he went out and wept most bitterly: Matthew 26:75

For which of you, desiring to build a tower, does not first sit down and count the cost, whether he has enough to complete it? Otherwise, when he has laid a foundation, and is not able to finish, all who see it begin to mock him, saying, 'This man began to build, and was not able to finish.': Luke 14: 28-30

...we ascend only such towers as we ourselves are able to build: Osip Mandelstam, "The Morning of Acmeism," *Mandelstam*, Cambridge University Press, 1973, p. 146, tr. Clarence Brown

But if my love for you could only help: *SMP*, Recitative 19 (25), ll. 12-14, p. 68

The *Passion*-sound

I used a stairway which nearly had ceased to exist: Anna Maria Ortese, "Where Time is Another," from *A Music Behind the Wall*, Selected Stories Vol. 2, 1997, tr. Henry Martin

Come ye daughters, help me, help me mourn (Kommt ihr Töchter, helft mir klagen): *SMP*, Chorus 1, line 1, p. 1

But He has done us only good (Er hat uns allen wohlgetan): *SMP*, Recitative 48 (57), line 1, p. 202

What shall I tell my soul (Ach, was soll ich der Seele sagen): *SMP*, Aria 30, Part 2, line 9, p. 141

Workshop Instruments

For as soon as the wind goeth over it, it is gone, and the place thereof shall know it no more: Psalm 103:16

Herzliebster Jesu

The fairest order in the world is but a heap of random sweepings: Heraclitus, *The Art and Thought of Heraclitus,* Cambridge University Press, 1979, Fragment CXXV, p. 85, tr. Charles H. Kahn

Herzliebster Jesu, was hast Du verbrochen: Johann Heermann, stanza 1, line 1, p. 22

The kingdom isn't something you can see…: Luke 17:20-21

Builders of Instruments

And tongueless I can still pronounce your name.: Rainer Maria Rilke, *Poems from the Book of Hours*, New Directions, 1975, tr. Babette Deutsch, adapted with changes by the author

The women who had followed him, and stayed with him and stood, and from afar off were beholding…: Matthew 27:55, (also in *SMP*, Recitative 63c, p. 266)

Aus Liebe

Aus Liebe will mein Heiland sterben (Out of love): *SMP*, Aria 49 (58), line 1, p. 204

Each of us must bear our part: Chris Zimmerman, "Bach's Great Passion, An Appreciation," *Plough* (online), 3.19.21

He has cast out every sickness: Matthew 8:16

Ich lebte mit der Welt in Lust und Freuden,
und du musst Leiden!
(For my joy and pleasure,
While Thou must suffer):
Johann Heermann, "Herzliebster Jesu," stanza 7, lines 3-4

Bethany

Du lieber Heiland du: SMP, Recitativo, Aria 5 (9), line 1, p. 33

Buss und Reu: *SMP*, Aria 6 (10), line 1 p. 34

Cataract Surgery, 1750

I come to the end — I am still with you: Psalm 139:18

We sit down in tears…
We call to you, rest Thou,
my Jesus softly rest
(Wir setzen uns mit Tränen nieder
Und rufen dir im Grabe zu:
Ruhe sanfte, sanfte ruh!):
SMP, Chorus, 68 (78), lines 1-3, pp. 293-94

Mary and the other Mary: "Mary Magdalene and the other Mary were there, sitting opposite the tomb." Matthew 27:61

World, go away
(Welt, geh aus):
SMP, Aria 65 (75), line 6, p. 276

On every side… the crowns of kings… were heaped: Tablet 7, *The Epic of Gilgamesh,* Stanford University Press, 1990, tr. by Maureen Gallery Kovacs. Ellipses are the author's

And without any feet can go to you: Rainer Maria Rilke, *Poems from the Book of Hours*, New Directions, 1975, tr. Babette Deutsch

ACKNOWLEDGMENTS

I wish to thank Bach scholar Christoph Wolff for his kind help in swiftly answering my questions along the way; and Dr. Gary Smith, former President of the American Academy in Berlin, and Barbara Schneider-Kempf, former Director General of the Staats Biblitotek zu Berlin, because of whose surpassing generosity I was invited to see Bach's manuscript of the *St. Matthew Passion*.

Grateful acknowledgement is made to the publications in which the following poems first appeared in 2024:

"Aus Liebe" in *Irish Pages: War in Europe*.
"A Rising Minor Sixth", "Herzliebster Jesu", and "Bethany" in *New American Studies: A Forum*, University of Göttingen.

ABOUT THE AUTHOR

 Gjertrud Schnackenberg was born in Tacoma, Washington, in 1953. Her awards include fellowships from the Guggenheim Foundation, the National Endowment for the Arts, the Rome Prize in Literature from the American Academy and Institute of Arts and Letters, the American Academy in Berlin, the Radcliffe Institute for Advanced Study at Harvard University, and an Award in Literature from the American Academy of Arts and Letters. She has been a Christensen Visiting Fellow at St. Catherine's College, Oxford, and a Visiting Scholar at the Getty Research Institute for the History of Art and the Humanites. *The Throne of Labdacus* received the 2001 *Los Angeles Times* Book Prize in Poetry, and *Heavenly Questions* received the 2011 Griffin International Prize for Poetry.

Books by

A R R O W S M I T H

PRESS

Girls by Oksana Zabuzhko

Bula Matari/Smasher of Rocks by Tom Sleigh

This Carrying Life by Maureen McLane

Cries of Animals Dying by Lawrence Ferlinghetti

Animals in Wartime by Matiop Wal

Divided Mind by George Scialabba

The Jinn by Amira El-Zein

Bergstein
edited by Askold Melnyczuk

Arrow Breaking Apart by Jason Shinder

Beyond Alchemy by Daniel Berrigan

Conscience, Consequence: Reflections on Father Daniel Berrigan
edited by Askold Melnyczuk

Ric's Progress by Donald Hall

Return To The Sea by Etnairis Rivera

The Kingdom of His Will by Catherine Parnell

cont...

ARROWSMITH is named after the late William Arrowsmith, a renowned classics scholar, literary and film critic. General editor of thirty-three volumes of *The Greek Tragedy in New Translations*, he was also a brilliant translator of Eugenio Montale, Cesare Pavese, and others. Arrowsmith, who taught for years in Boston University's University Professors Program, championed not only the classics and the finest in contemporary literature, he was also passionate about the importance of recognizing the translator's role in bringing the original work to life in a new language.

Like the arrowsmith who turns his arrows straight and true, a wise person makes his character straight and true.

— Buddha